THE SKELETAL SYSTEM

Frameworks for Life

THE SKELETAL SYSTEM
Frameworks for Life

Dr. Alvin Silverstein
and
Virginia B. Silverstein

Illustrated by Lee J. Ames

PRENTICE-HALL, INC., Englewood Cliffs, N.J.

For Shirley and Sam Piltz

THE SKELETAL SYSTEM: Frameworks for Life by
Dr. Alvin Silverstein and Virginia B. Silverstein

Printed in the United States of America

Prentice-Hall International, Inc., London
Prentice-Hall of Australia, Pty. Ltd., North Sydney
Prentice-Hall of Canada, Ltd., Toronto
Prentice-Hall of India Private Ltd., New Delhi
Prentice-Hall of Japan, Inc., Tokyo

Library of Congress Cataloging in Publication Data
Silverstein, Alvin.
    The skeletal system.
    SUMMARY: Analyzes the structure and function of the
human skeletal system and compares it with that of other
animals.
    1. Skeleton. [1. Skeleton] I. Silverstein,
Virginia B., joint author. II. Title.
QM101.S45   612'.75   71-39146
ISBN 0-13-812701-8

10   9   8   7   6   5

Contents

1
Frameworks for Life

Have you ever made a kite? You start out with two thin strips of wood. These will serve as the framework that will hold the paper body of the kite firm and stiff. The house you live in may also have a framework of wood. Or perhaps you live in a big apartment house, which has a framework of steel girders. Cars and buses, boats and airplanes, all have an inner framework that helps to support them and hold their basic shape.

Your body, too, has an inner framework. It is called the *skeleton,* and it is made of bones. Feel your fingers. You can feel the hard bones inside. Squeeze your arms and legs and press down on the top of your head. There are firm bones under the skin in nearly all parts of your body.

Dogs and cats, mice and elephants, frogs and snakes all have skeletons made of bones, very much

like ours. In all these animals the skeleton is an
inner framework, covered by layers of soft flesh.
Many members of the animal kingdom have a
different kind of skeleton—a skeleton on the *outside*. Insects and spiders, lobsters and crayfish all
have an outer skeleton made like a jointed suit of
armor. Clams and snails have hard limy shells
that form a framework on the outside.

The shell of a snail, like the frame of a house, is
a very solid structure. It cannot bend back and
forth. But the skeletons of most living things are
very flexible. Bend your arm, roll your head about,
curl your fingers into a ball and then stretch them.

Bones themselves are rather hard. Why isn't the skeleton stiff and rigid like the framework of a house? The flexibility come from the way the bones are put together. The beams of a house are all nailed firmly together. Bones are held in place by bands of tough tissues called *ligaments* (LIG-UH-MENTS) and *tendons*. These connections permit the bones to move about with some freedom.

How does a bone move? Bones cannot move by themselves. They are pulled by *muscles*. Indeed, muscles not only move bones, but they also help to keep them in the proper positions when they are not moving. The wood frame of a house provides the support for the walls and floors and roof, but the bones of the body do not provide *all* the support for the skin and soft tissues and organs. It is the bones, working together with the muscles, that provide support for our bodies.

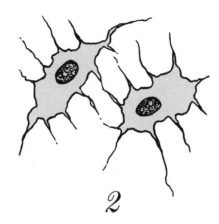

2

Connective Tissue

Our bodies are made of a number of different kinds of tissues. Covering tissue forms the skin that covers the outside of the body and the linings that cover the inner parts. Nerve tissue carries messages that help us to think and see and feel, and also tell the parts of the body exactly what to do and when to do it. Muscle tissue provides the pulling forces that move the body parts. All these tissues are held together, or connected, by several types of tissues called *connective tissue*. Bones are made of one type of connective tissue. Another type forms the tendons and ligaments that connect muscles to bones and hold the bones together in joints. Have you ever noticed rubbery pieces of gristle in meat? These are made of another type of connective tissue, called *cartilage* (CAR-TIH-LEDJ).

What would happen if all the connective tissue in your body were suddenly, magically to disap-

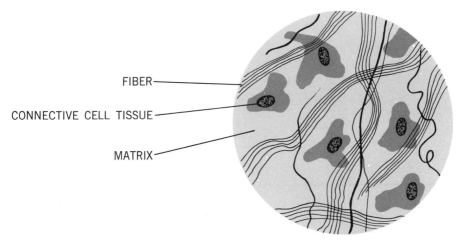

FIBER

CONNECTIVE CELL TISSUE

MATRIX

Microscopic view of fibrous connective tissue.

pear? You would tumble down instantly into a shapeless heap. For it is the connective tissue that gives the body its basic shape by supporting and holding the other tissues together.

Each connective tissue cell produces a large amount of a nonliving substance called *matrix* (MAY-TRIX). The matrix is found between the connective tissue cells and binds them together. It is the kind of matrix that determines what kind of connective tissue the cells form and what jobs they can do in the body.

One important type of connective tissue is called *fibrous* (FYE-BRUSS) *connective tissue,* because its matrix is a thickly criss-crossing network of protein fibers. These thread-like fibers are very thin—each so small that it cannot be seen without a microscope. There is a thick mat of fibrous connective tissue just under the skin. When this tissue is

5

treated with certain chemicals, it becomes tough and leathery. In fact, that is exactly what *leather* is—the skin of an animal with the thick layer of connective tissue underneath, toughened by treating it with chemicals in a process called *tanning*.

The protein in connective tissue fibers is called *collagen* (COLL-A-JEN). If these fibers are placed in hot water, the collagen changes. It turns into another protein called *gelatin* (JELL-A-TIN). Both collagen and gelatin are built from almost exactly the same amino acid building blocks.

Have you ever heard someone say that an old horse should be sent to the glue factory? One kind of glue is actually an impure form of gelatin. It is made by cooking the hides and bones of various animals, including old horses. The gelatin that you eat in desserts, jellied meats, and other foods is made in much the same way, only it is much purer and is made more carefully than glue.

Does your mother ever tell you to drink plenty of milk so that your bones will be strong? Milk is rich in *calcium* (KAL-SEE-UM), and so are bones. Part of the matrix of bone is made of mineral salts that contain calcium. Interwoven through the matrix are collagen fibers. It is the combination of protein fibers and mineral salts that gives bones their great strength.

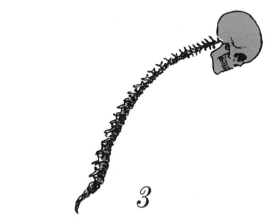

3

The Human Skeleton

Did you know that you have more bones than either your mother or father? Each of them has 206 bones. But you have dozens more. And you had even more when you were younger. Bend forward and feel along the middle of your back. Do you feel little bumps running down in a straight line beginning at your neck? They are the parts of your backbone called the *vertebrae* (VER-TEH-BRAY). How many can you count? You may have as many as 33, but an adult has only 26 vertebrae.

Bones do not disappear as you grow older. Indeed, some new bones appear. But meanwhile, many of the bones of your body grow together, or fuse, to form a single bone where there were two or more. That is just what happens to the vertebrae. When a baby is born there is a soft spot on the top of his head. That part it not protected by bone, and his brain could be damaged if he is hit there.

Gradually the bones of the skull grow together and close up the opening in the skull. By the time the baby is about two years old, all of his brain is protected by a covering of solid bone.

Scientists usually divide the human skeleton into two main groups of bones: the *axial* (AX-ee-al) *skeleton* and the *appendicular* (ap-pen-DICK-yew-lar) *skeleton*. The axial skeleton consists of the bones that run down the middle of the body, its *axis*. These are the *skull* or *cranium* (CRANE-ee-um), the vertebrae of the *backbone*, the *ribs*, and the *breastbone*. The term appendicular comes from a word meaning "to hang." The bones of the appendicular skeleton are attached to, or "hang" from the bones of the axial skeleton. These are the bones of the arms and legs and the heavy crosswise bones called girdles, that attach them to the axial skeleton.

The picture on page 9 shows the bones of the human skeleton, with the names of some of the most important bones. Each of the 206 bones of the adult skeleton has its own name, and medical students and nursing students must spend long hours memorizing all these names.

See how many of these bones you can find in your own body. Bones are so hard that you will be able to feel many of them clearly through your flesh. First feel around your head. There is a hard bony helmet protecting your brain: the cranium.

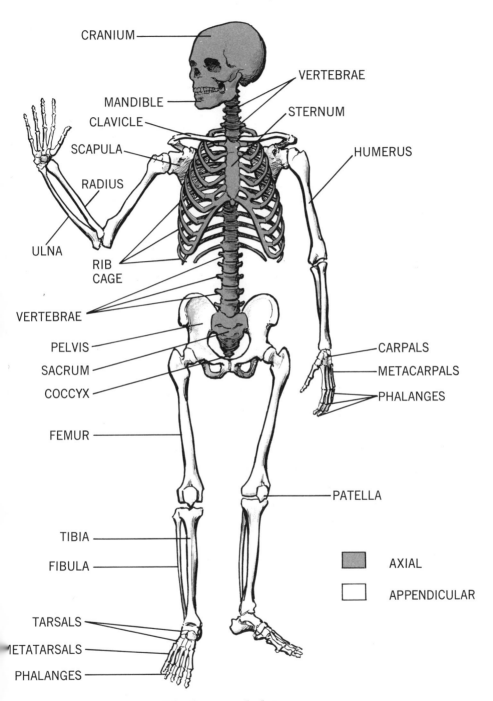

CRANIUM

VERTEBRAE

MANDIBLE

STERNUM

CLAVICLE

HUMERUS

SCAPULA

RADIUS

ULNA

RIB
CAGE

VERTEBRAE

PELVIS

CARPALS

SACRUM

METACARPALS

COCCYX

PHALANGES

FEMUR

PATELLA

TIBIA

FIBULA

AXIAL

APPENDICULAR

TARSALS

METATARSALS

PHALANGES

The human skeleton.

Can you feel any separate bones? Although the skull starts out as a number of separate bones, these grow together as a baby grows. Feel carefully around your eyes. There are round openings in the face bones here—hollow eye sockets into which the eyeballs fit. There is another opening for the air passages of the nose. Spread your hands over your face and open your mouth wide. Which bone moved? It was the lower jaw bone, called the *mandible* (MAN-DIH-BUL). Trace its outline with your fingers. The mandible is the largest, strongest bone of the face.

Has anyone ever told you to straighten up your spine? Yet the vertebral column is not really straight, like a broomstick, at all. It is shaped like a long S-curve. See if you can feel the curves of your backbone. It comes out from the neck, over the broad part of the back, then curves in to the small of the back, and out again. You can see this more clearly if you look at someone else's back. The curves of the vertebral column make it easier to balance in an upright position, with the least possible strain from the weights of the head and body parts. Indeed, an infant's spine *is* straight. It is only when he begins to hold his head up by himself and then to sit and stand that the S-curves of the spine develop.

Just as the brain is enclosed in a protective helmet of bone, so the heart and lungs are also protected by a bony framework, the ribs. But the skull is solid bone, and the ribs form a cage of separate bones, with spaces between them. Feel along the front of your chest, and trace the outlines of your rib cage. How many ribs can you count? They come in pairs, one on each side, and there are twenty-four ribs (twelve pairs) altogether. The upper seven pairs of ribs are attached directly to a flat, dagger-shaped bone called the breastbone or *sternum* (STER-num). You can feel the sternum in the middle of your chest.

What are the two bones that stick out on the upper part of the chest, just below the neck? These are the collar bones, or *clavicles* (CLAV-ih-kls). What about the two bones that stick out like "wings" on the upper back, just below the shoulders? These are part of the shoulder blades or *scapulas* (SCAP-yew-luhs). The clavicles and scapulas together form the shoulder girdles that attach the arm bones to the axial skeleton.

How many long bones do you have in each arm? You can feel one thick bone running the length of your upper arm. This is called the *humerus* (HEW-mer-us). But in the forearm there are two separate long bones. You can feel the dividing space between them most easily near the wrist. The longer bone on the side of the little finger is called the *ulna* (ULL-nuh), and the slightly shorter bone on the thumb side is called the *radius* (RAY-dee-us).

You may be able to feel a number of small, knobby bones in your wrist. These are called *carpals* (CAR-PULZ). Exactly how many carpals you have will depend on how old you are. A baby has no carpals at all, but by the time you are grown, you will have eight carpals in each hand. Five long bones, called *metacarpals* (MET-UH-CAR-PULZ), form the framework of the palm of the hand. The bones of the fingers are called *phalanges* (FUH-LANJ-EEZ). How many can you feel? There are three in each finger, but only two in the thumb.

Just below the waist, you can feel the tops of your hip bones. These large bones form the *pelvic girdle* that attaches the leg bones to the lower part of the spine. The set of leg bones is very much like the bones of the arm. A single long, heavy bone forms the framework for the upper leg. This is called the *femur* (FEE-mur). The lower leg has two long bones, the *tibia* (TIB-EE-UH) or shin bone, and the *fibula* (FIB-YEW-LUH). At the joint between the upper and lower leg is the *patella* (PA-TELL-UH) or kneecap. A collection of short bones, the *tarsals* (TAR-SULZ), form the heel and part of the foot. The long bones of the foot are called *metatarsals* (MET-UH-TAR-SULZ). And the toe bones, just like the finger bones, are called phalanges.

Which is the longest bone in the body? Measure all the long parts of your arms and legs to see.

12

Using the picture on page 9 as a model, draw the outlines of the major bones of the skeleton on a sheet of cardboard and cut them out carefully. Attach the bones together in the proper order with a needle and thread. Now you have a model of the human skeleton. Try to stand it up. It will promptly collapse. This is what would happen to a real human skeleton, standing by itself. In your body, muscles support the bones and help them to move. You can provide "muscle power" for your model skeleton by attaching strings to the skull, shoulder, arm, and leg bones. Now you can move the cardboard bones somewhat as muscles move the real bones of your arms and legs.

Rub the palms of your hands together rapidly. Notice how warm they get. The heat is produced by friction as the two hands rub against each other. Friction produces heat when any two surfaces rub together. The rougher the surfaces are, the more heat is produced.

The ends of the bones rub against each other each time they move. If these ends were rough, our joints would get very hot, and it would hurt every time we move. The constant friction would cause the ends of the bones to wear down. But this does not happen because the ends of the bones are covered with a smooth, slippery coating of cartilage.

Lubricants can also help to cut down on the fric-

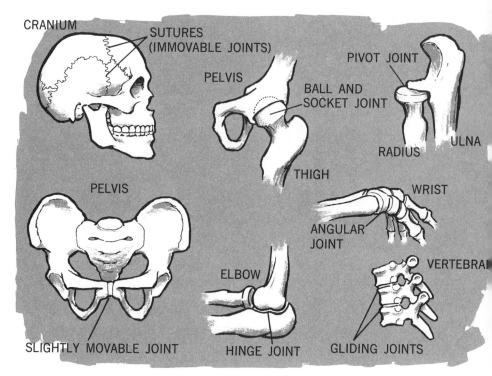

Bones are connected in various kinds of joints.

tion of moving parts. Your bike has to be oiled regularly to run smoothly. So does a car or any other machine with moving parts. There is a lubricant in the joints of the bones, too. It is called *synovial* (SIH-NOH-VEE-UL) fluid. This lubricant is not an oil or grease. It is more like the watery saliva in your mouth. Older people often do not have as much synovial fluid in their joints. That is why they may find moving difficult.

There are a number of different kinds of joints in the body. Make a fist with one hand. Cup the fingers of the other hand around it. You have a *ball-and-socket joint.* You can turn the ball of your fist freely in any direction within the socket formed by the other hand. Ball-and-socket joints provide the most freedom of movement of any type of joint. The joints in your shoulders and hips are of this type. You can swing your arm or leg around in a full circle.

Another kind of joint is the *hinge joint* that works something like the hinge on a door. Your knees and elbows have hinge joints. They can only move back and forth.

Move your thumb back and forth. Now move it up and down, and around in a circle. What kind of a joint connects your thumb bones to your hand? You can move your thumb more freely than you can move the parts of your arms and legs connected at your elbow and knee joints, so it is not a hinge joint. Yet you do not have quite as much freedom as a ball-and-socket joint provides. The kind of joint that is found in your thumb is called a *saddle joint,* because it is shaped something like a saddle.

Some joints do not permit any movement at all. The bones of your skull are held together in firm joints called *sutures* (SUE-CHERS). Can you feel any of them? How many of your joints can you find? Count them.

4
Bone Cells and
Bone Structure

Look at a thigh bone from a chicken or turkey. It is long and thin, with large knobs on each end. Notice the gristle attached to the ends of the bones. This is the slippery cartilage that helps to cut down on friction in the joints. The top knob, with its cartilage cover, is rounded. It is part of a ball-and-socket joint. The other end is shaped something like a spool. It is part of a hinge joint.

Try to bend the bone. It is hard and firm and does not bend. And yet it is rather light—much lighter than a metal bar of the same size would be. One reason why bones are surprisingly light for their size is that they are not solid.

Take a saw and cut across the middle of the bone. Notice that the solid bone forms only a thin rim. A soft, spongy, reddish substance fills up most of the hollow inside the bone. This is the *bone marrow*.

Now take another thigh bone and place it in a covered jar filled with vinegar. After a few days, pour out the vinegar, wash off the bone, and look at it. Try bending it. Then put it back in the jar and add fresh vinegar. Do the same thing again every few days. You will notice that the bone is becoming flexible. You will be able to bend it more and more. After a few weeks it will still be the same size and shape it started out, but it will now be like a rubber bone. You could almost tie it into a knot.

What happened to the bone? Vinegar is a weak acid, and it dissolved out the minerals from the bone. The protein part of the matrix does not dissolve in vinegar. And so it remained to hold the shape of the original bone. It is still strong, but it is very flexible. It was the mineral salts that made the bone rigid.

You can make some models that will illustrate how the two parts of the bone matrix give bone its special properties. Take a piece of cheesecloth and roll it into a tube. Cheesecloth is a mesh of cotton fibers, much like the network of protein fibers in the bone matrix. The cheesecloth tube will not break easily, but it will quickly flatten out. It will not hold a firm shape.

Now seal off the end of an empty cardboard tube from a roll of paper towels or toilet paper. Fill the tube with plaster of Paris, mixed with water in the right proportions to make a plaster model. When the plaster hardens, peel off the cardboard mold. Now you have a plaster cylinder, something like a long bone. It is firm and rigid, but it is not strong. You can break the plaster rod easily, just by bending it with your hands.

Now place a roll of cheesecloth several layers thick inside another carboard tube and fill that with plaster of Paris. When the plaster sets, you will have a plaster rod that looks just like the other one. But layers of cheesecloth will be embedded inside. You will find it much harder to break this rod. The plaster gives it shape, and the network of fibers strengthens it.

Just how strong is bone? It is stronger than most man-made materials, even stronger than the structural steel that forms the framework of huge skyscrapers. Indeed, one of the important problems researchers had to solve in designing artificial replacements for bones damaged so badly in accidents that they could not be repaired, was to find strong enough materials. When they tried to make a stainless steel femur the same size as a normal femur made of bone, it snapped under the normal loads of standing and walking. Special alloys had to be invented, and even they were not as good as the amazing natural substance, bone. Our leg bones can stand up to a force of one ton without snapping or bending.

Why must bones be so strong? They must hold

up the weight of the body in normal activities, and they must also be able to withstand special emergency loads. When you jump down the steps or off a wall, you are putting a tremendous force on your leg bones when you land.

Look closely at the cut surface of the thigh bone that you sawed in half. The outer ring of hard bone looks all the same. It is very dense, with no spaces or gaps in it. Even if you look at it through a magnifying glass, the surface of this bone will still look smooth and dense. This type of bony tissue is called *compact bone.*

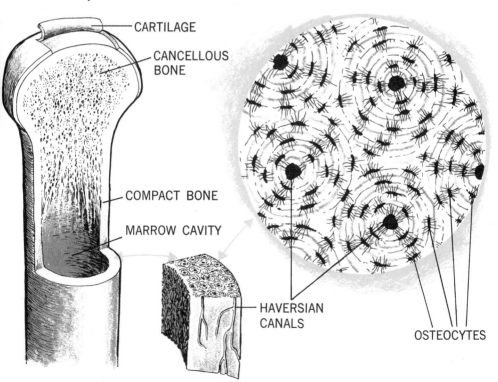

The structure of bones.

Now saw through one of the bone pieces again, this time in the knobby end part. Look at this new cut surface. There is an outer ring of compact bone, but inside it there is a layer that looks like a lacy network of bone with many small spaces inside. It looks rather like the cut edge of a sponge. This kind of bone is called *spongy bone* or *cancellous* (CAN-sell-us) *bone*. (Cancellous comes from a Latin word that means "covered with bars.") Cancellous bone is nearly as strong as compact bone, but it is much lighter, for part of it is just empty space.

Bone seems nonliving, like a stone. And indeed, the matrix of bone is made of nonliving substances. The mineral part is made of a type of calcium phosphate, a salt containing the elements calcium and phosphorus. The protein fibers are also nonliving, like the proteins in your hair and nails. (When you cut your fingernails or hair, you do not bleed or feel anything.) But if you could cut a very thin slice of bone and look at it under a microscope, you would see that there are numerous living bone cells, called *osteocytes* (OSS-tee-oh-sytes) embedded between layers of hard bony tissue. (The name of the osteocytes comes from words meaning "bone" and "cell.") The bony substance itself is arranged in long cylinders, nested one inside another. These groups of cylinders are called *haversian* (HA-VER-SHAN) *systems.* (Like many parts of the body, these structures are named after the man who first described them.) The rings that you see when you cut across an onion look very much the way the cut edge of a haversian system looks under a microscope. There are usually fewer than six layers of bony substance in each system. The osteocytes are found in small hollows between the bony cylinders, and there is a hollow central channel in the middle of the smallest cylinder. This central channel is called a *haversian canal.* Within the haversian canal is one or more blood vessels, for bone cells, like all other living cells, need a constant supply of oxygen and food materials; their carbon dioxide and other waste products must be carried away continually by the bloodstream, or they will die. Side branches of blood vessels cut through from the covering of the bone. Materials are carried in and out of the bones through these blood vessels.

Have you ever had a broken arm? Your arm swelled up and hurt terribly. At first the doctor might not have been sure whether the bone was broken, or it was just a bad bruise. He took an X-ray to make sure. X-rays are radiations just as light rays are. We cannot see X-rays, but they do show up on photographic film. They can pass easily through the soft tissues of the body, but bone

An X-ray picture shows the doctor where the bone is broken.

stops them. And so in an X-ray picture the bones are clearly outlined. The doctor can see exactly where the break or *fracture* is. With the X-ray picture to guide him, the doctor was able to set the fracture. He moved the arm until the broken ends of the bone were neatly fitted together.

In time, broken bones can grow back together so well that the bone is just as strong as it was before. But for a fracture to heal properly, the broken parts of the bone must be held perfectly still. If they are allowed to move, they may come apart again, or they may grow together crookedly. That is why a doctor places a broken arm in a *cast,* a casing of plaster that fits snugly around the arm and prevents it from moving.

Almost immediately after the bone is set, it begins to heal. Special bone-forming cells, called *osteoblasts* (OSS-TEE-OH-BLASTS), move from the outer layers of the old bone into the gap between the broken ends. These cells produce the protein form of the matrix and help to form a bridge across the gap. Soon calcium salts appear in the matrix. New bone is growing; it is still rather soft. This new growth joining the broken ends is called a *callus* (KAL-us). Day by day, more bone cells are formed and produce more matrix. Gradually the callus hardens to form true bone.

It takes a long time for a bone to heal. Exactly how long it will take depends on many things. A young child's bones will heal faster than an older person's. Arm bones heal faster than leg bones. If the broken parts of the bone are pressed tightly together, they will heal faster than if they are not so tight. A broken arm takes a month or more to grow together; in an older person, one of the large leg bones may take as long as six months to heal.

Recently a team of surgeons at the University of Pennsylvania reported on a new technique that can speed up the healing of broken bones. Studies of rabbit bones had shown that there is a small negative electric charge on the growing ends of bones. The middle parts of the bones tend to be electrically neutral or even positive. But if a bone is broken, the whole surface of the bone becomes negative, with the strongest negative charge at the break. This charge does not disappear until the fracture is completely healed. The researchers reasoned that the electric charge must have something to do with the healing process. So they tried applying very small electric currents to broken bones. The bones healed much faster than they normally would. After working out the right current strength in experiments on rabbits, the medical team tried the technique on human patients, with excellent success. Not only do broken bones heal in half the time with electric current, but there is much less damage to the muscles attached to the bones, which tend to shrivel and stiffen if an arm or leg is kept in a cast for many months.

5
How Bones Work

Can you lift a ten pound bag of potatoes? Probably you can, but you will find it hard work. Here's a way to make it easier: Tie a string around the top of the bag and make a loop in the free end. Lift the potatoes onto a chair. Place the end of a mop handle through the loop of string and rest the handle on the back of the chair. Now press down on the other end of the mop handle, far away from the bag. It is much easier to lift the potatoes this way. You have made a model of a *lever*. This is a simple machine that helps to increase the force you can exert.

Your arm and leg bones and other long bones in your body work as levers. They are like the mop handle lever you used to increase your strength in lifting the potatoes. But a lever does not work unless a force is applied to it. Muscles supply the force that moves the bones of the body.

Bend your arm up and "make a muscle." Feel the bulge in your upper arm. This is a muscle called the *biceps* (BYE-seps) muscle. It is pulling on a bone in your lower arm, the radius. Now feel the calf of your leg. Stand up on your toes. The large muscle in your calf becomes even larger and firmer. This muscle is called the *gastrocnemius* (GAS-TRUK-NEE-MEE-US) muscle. It pulls on the heel bone.

The muscles that work with the bones of the skeleton are called *skeletal muscles.* A skeletal muscle is usually a spindle-shaped bundle of millions of individual muscle fibers. These fibers are able to contract, thus becoming much shorter.

Skeletal muscles work in pairs. If you had only a biceps muscle attached to your lower arm, once you bent it up you would not be able to straighten

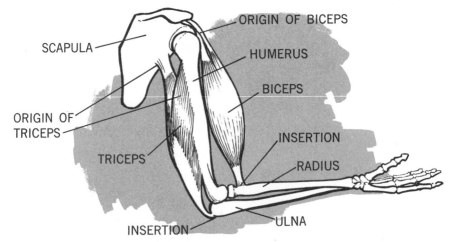

Bones and muscles work together to move the arm.

it out again. You would have to wait until the muscle slowly relaxed. But there is another muscle attached to the bones of the lower arm. This muscle is called the *triceps* (TRYE-SEPS) muscle. It is attached to the ulna, the bone on the little finger side. When the triceps contracts, it pulls on the ulna and straightens the arm.

Muscles are attached to the bones by thick, tough cords of connective tissue called tendons. Look at the back of your hand while you move your fingers up and down. Narrow bands, running from the fingers up to the wrist, are raised and lowered as your fingers move. These are tendons. You can feel a particularly large tendon at the back of your leg, just above the heel. This tendon attaches the gastrocnemius muscle to the heel bone. It is called the *Achilles* (A-KILL-EEZ) *tendon*. Its name comes from a Greek myth. According to the story, when the warrior Achilles was a baby, his mother held him by the heel and dipped him into the river Styx. The water of this river had the magical power to make a man invulnerable. When Achilles grew up, no blow could harm him—it was as though he was covered with an invisible shield. But he had a secret weak point. The waters of the river had not touched a small part of the back of his heel, where his mother had held him. Achilles was finally slain by an arrow at this one vulnerable spot. Now people often refer to a weak point as an "Achilles' heel." The Achilles tendon is a vulnerable part of the body indeed. If it is cut or torn, the use of the leg is lost immediately.

Bones are fastened to other bones by bands of a different kind of connective tissue called ligaments. Their name comes from a word meaning "to tie." Ligaments are very similar to tendons, but they are more flexible. This flexibility helps to give the bones freedom of movement in the joints.

Muscles help bones to support the body. Through the teamwork of muscles and bones, coordinated by messages sent through the nervous system, we are able to walk, run, and jump, eat, talk, and write. Muscles and bones are working together as we throw a ball or swim. We could not even stand or sit without the support that they provide.

Supporting the body is not the only job that bones do. Football players wear special helmets to protect their heads from injury when they are tackled. Construction workers wear "hard hats" to protect them from objects that might fall on their heads. Baseball players also put on hard batting helmets when they go up to bat. For special situations like these, extra protection is necessary to protect the head from injury. But under most conditions your brain is protected quite well by the helmet you are already "wearing." This is the hard bony skull or cranium.

The brain is one of the most important organs in the body. If it is destroyed, death will follow in a matter of minutes. Even if it is slightly damaged, important abilities—speech or sight or movement—may be lost. Yet the brain is a mass of soft tissue, extremely delicate. Without the protection that the skull provides, the brain could be damaged by the slightest bump or blow.

The spinal cord is also very delicate, and nearly as important as the brain. Messages from the brain travel along this white bundle of nerves to various parts of the body. Some of our movements are made in response to messages from the spinal cord, without involving the brain at all. The spinal cord has its own bony protection, the spine or vertebral

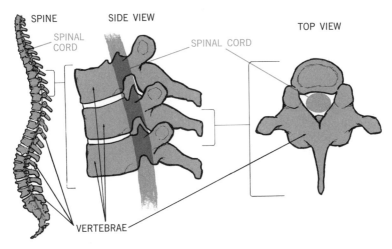

The spinal cord is protected by the flexible tube formed by the vertebrae.

column. The bony sheath around the spinal cord is quite different from the helmet-like cranium that protects the brain. The skull is rigid and unmoving. But what would happen if you had a rigid spine, made of a cylinder of solid bone as straight and stiff as a water pipe? That kind of spine would protect your spinal cord very nicely, but you would not be able to bend at all. Instead, the spine is made of a series of small bones, the vertebrae, which fit neatly together to form a flexible column that permits you to bend and turn with ease.

Other bones also help to protect soft organs of the body. The ribs, for example, form a bony cage that shelters the heart and lungs. The pelvis, or hip bones, help to protect the organs in the lower part of the body. And safely sheltered inside hollows of the bones themselves is the bone marrow, the soft tissue where the blood cells are produced.

Support and protection—these are the functions that most people think of when the bones are mentioned. But the skeleton has another job that is just as important as these two. It serves as a storehouse for calcium and phosphorus. These two minerals are very important in the workings of the body. Phosphorus is a key part of the *nucleic* (NEW-CLAY-ik) *acids,* DNA and RNA. These chemicals carry the blueprints for life, the hereditary information that determines how we are formed, and controls nearly every chemical reaction that goes on in the body. Calcium is needed for the muscles to work properly. There must be a certain amount of it in the blood and body fluids at all times. Otherwise the muscles will all contract suddenly and violently.

We tend to think of bones as nonliving, unchanging structures, like a stone. But this is not really so. Chemicals are constantly being added to and taken away from the bones. If you do not eat foods with enough calcium and phosphorus, your body will take whatever it needs of these minerals from your bones and teeth. If too much calcium is taken out of the bones, they become soft and bendable. Then the weight of the body and the pull of the muscles may push some of the long bones out of shape. Have you ever heard a woman say that she loses a tooth every time she has a baby? She probably does not drink milk or eat cheeses and other foods rich in calcium. When she is pregnant, the baby growing inside her needs plenty of calcium and phosphorus to build its bones; since she is not taking in a sufficient supply of these minerals with the foods she eats, they are taken out of her own bones and teeth to supply the baby's needs.

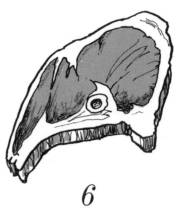

6

Within the Bones

The human body is a wonder of compact efficiency. Nearly thirty feet of intestines are neatly coiled and folded into a space no larger than a bucket. The linings of the air pockets of the lungs together could cover the whole roof of a house. The body organs are neatly packed together; little space is wasted. Even the hollows inside the bones are used to good advantage. They are filled with spongy bone marrow.

The bone marrow is an important part of the circulatory system. It is here that the blood cells —both red cells and white cells—are made. The red cells are formed in the reddish masses of tissue known as *red bone marrow*. Many of the white blood cells of the body are also produced here. The next time you eat a lamb chop with a round bone, look carefully at it. Feel the soft, spongy material inside the hole. This is bone marrow.

Before you go to sleep tonight, billions of red blood cells in your body will die. But at the same time, billions of new red cells will be formed to take their place. A grown man may have as many as 25,000,000,000,000 red blood cells in his body. Each one lives about four months.

There is something rather strange about red blood cells. They are the only cells in the human body that do not have nuclei. The red blood cells do not start out that way. When they are first formed in the red bone marrow, each one has a nucleus—a rather large one, in fact. The red blood cell is formed from a bone marrow cell called a *stem cell*. As the new red cell develops in the bone marrow, it goes through a series of stages. The red pigment *hemoglobin* (HEE-MOH-GLOH-BIN) is produced in the maturing cells, and gives the red bone marrow its color. Gradually the nucleus

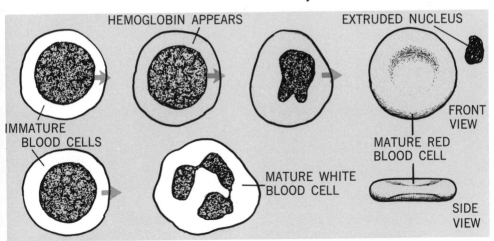

Stem cells in the bone marrow develop into red and white blood cells.

breaks down and finally disappears entirely. At last the mature red blood cell squeezes in through a tiny pore in one of the blood capillaries that run through the bones and takes its place in the blood-stream. There its hemoglobin will help it to carry oxygen from the lungs to the cells of the body and carry the cells' waste carbon dioxide back to the lungs.

The stem cells of the red bone marrow can also form white blood cells. These colorless cells are the body's disease fighters. They creep and swim along the blood and lymph vessels and roam through the tissues, capturing bacteria and other invaders. There are about seven hundred red cells for every white cell in the blood. Some of the white cells are formed in the red bone marrow. Others are produced in the lymph nodes and spleen.

Red bone marrow, producing red and white blood cells, fills the hollows of most of the bones of your body. There are also some portions of *yellow bone marrow,* which is used to store fat and does not make blood cells. In the teen years, the marrow of the long bones of the arms and legs grows more and more fatty. By the time you are about twenty, your long bones will be filled with yellow bone marrow. Only the marrow of other bones, such as your ribs, vertebrae, and sternum, will still be producing red and white blood cells.

If the bone marrow does not produce enough

red blood cells to replace the ones that are destroyed or lost, a condition called *anemia* (A-NEE-MEE-UH) results. Without enough red cells in the blood, the body cells do not get enough oxygen. The person feels tired all the time and does not have the energy to work and play as normal people do. Anemia can be caused by various things. Vitamins and minerals, especially iron, are needed to build red blood cells. If you do not get enough of these in your food, you may suffer from anemia. Certain diseases and poisons may cause anemia. So does a large loss of blood from a wound or operation. The blood that is lost contains both liquid and red and white blood cells. The body replaces the liquid very quickly—within a day or so if the person drinks enough fluids. But it takes longer for the bone marrow to replace the missing blood cells. Chemical signals in the blood tell the bone marrow that the tissues of the body are suffering from a lack of oxygen. Stem cells mature more quickly and in larger numbers than usual. Some regions of yellow bone marrow may even turn red and begin producing blood cells again until the emergency is over.

Anemia will also result from damage to the bone marrow. When atom bombs were dropped on Hiroshima and Nagasaki near the end of the Second World War, thousands of people in these cities were killed in the blast. But many of those who survived, died about a month later from anemia. Gamma radiations from the bombs destroyed their bone marrow. As their red and white blood cells died, there were no new ones to replace them.

Gamma rays destroy mainly the blood cells that have begun to develop. They do not do as much damage to the stem cells. And so, if people exposed to radiations can live through the first few months of anemia, their blood will eventually return to normal as the stem cells develop into new blood cells. Transplants of bone marrow cells are now used to help radiation victims. These transplants provide healthy new blood cells to help the victim through the emergency.

The X-rays that a doctor uses to take pictures of broken bones are radiations very much like gamma rays. But the doses of X-rays used for diagnosing bone fractures, tuberculosis, and other conditions are too small to harm the bone marrow and other tissues of the body. Indeed, both X-rays and gamma rays are used in larger doses to treat certain diseases. For example, these radiations can be used to destroy cancer cells to prevent them from multiplying and spreading through the body. When radiations are used in medical treatments, a lead shield is placed over some of the patient's large bones to protect the bone marrow inside.

Explosions of atomic weapons have created new

dangers of exposure to radiation that did not exist before. Radioactive elements tend to break down, sending out radiations as they are changed into other forms. Many of the radioactive substances that are released when a nuclear device explodes, break down within hours or days after the explosion and are not a problem any longer. But some radioactive substances break down more slowly. One of these is a form called *strontium 90*. This form or *isotope* (EYE-soh-TOHP) of the element strontium is produced in large amounts in atomic explosions. It has a *half-life* of twenty-eight years. This means that if you start out with a pound of strontium 90, half of it will *decay* or break down in twenty-eight years, and at the end of that time there will be only half a pound of the radioactive form left. After another twenty-eight years, a quarter pound of radioactive strontium will remain. The amount will continue to decrease by half each twenty-eight years, as the isotope decays.

Strontium is a chemical element that behaves very similarly to calcium. When the dust from an atomic explosion falls on soil, it is taken up into grass and other plants. If cows eat grass contaminated with strontium 90, this isotope passes into their milk, along with calcium. When people drink the milk from such a cow, some strontium 90 passes into their bones. And there it stays, sending

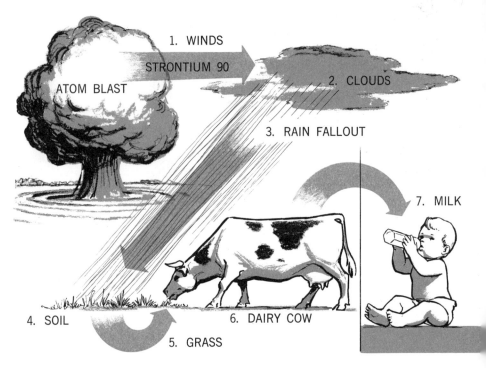

1. WINDS

STRONTIUM 90

ATOM BLAST

2. CLOUDS

3. RAIN FALLOUT

7. MILK

4. SOIL

5. GRASS

6. DAIRY COW

Strontium 90 from radioactive fallout, finds its way into human bones through food chains.

radiations into the bone marrow and out into the soft tissues of the body, for years. It was because of such dangers that most of the great powers of the world agreed to a Nuclear Test Ban Treaty, outlawing the testing of nuclear weapons in the earth's atmosphere.

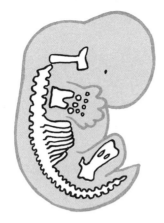

Cartilage, Bone, and How A Baby Grows

When your skeleton was first formed, while you were still in your mother's womb, it was not made of bone. Instead, it was made of soft, rubbery cartilage. Little by little the cartilage was replaced by bone. Even when you were born, much of your skeleton was still cartilage. This was a good thing, for the softness of your "bones" helped you to squeeze through the birth opening more easily. Perhaps your head looked a little lopsided for the first day or two. Your skull was still so soft that it was easily molded.

You grew very rapidly before you were born. In nine months you went from a tiny dot no bigger than a pinpoint to a miniature human about twenty inches long. After birth you continued to grow rapidly. In your first year you probably tripled your weight, and by the end of your second year you were already about half the height you

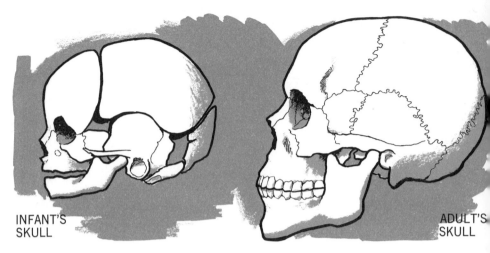

An adult has fewer bones than a child.

will be when you are an adult. Real bone filled in the cartilage "models" of your skeleton, and with this added support you were soon able to hold your head up, sit, stand, and walk. Your bones continued to grow, along with the rest of your body, and they are still growing. They will probably continue to grow until your middle or late teens, when you have reached your full height.

Bone is hard and firm. It does not stretch or bend. Much of it is made of minerals, just like a stone. How can it grow? When bone replaced the cartilage in your baby skeleton, not all of the cartilage disappeared. A cover of cartilage remained on the ends of the bones, helping to smooth the movements of the joints. And thin plates of cartilage remained where the large ends of the bone were joined to the thinner shaft or middle portion. The end portion of a long bone is

40

called the *epiphysis* (EH-PIFF-ih-sis). The shaft is called the *diaphysis* (DYE-AFF-ih-sis). The cartilage plate that separates these two parts is an important growth center. The cartilage cells on the side of the plate next to the epiphysis continually multiply, forming rows and columns of cartilage cells. On the other side of the plate, bone cells and blood vessels push into the cartilage and replace it. Calcium salts are deposited, and so new bone is formed. In this way the shafts of the bones grow longer. Finally, when you have finished growing, the cartilage cells in the growth plate stop multiplying. The cartilage is replaced by bone, and the growth plate disappears. The epiphysis and diaphysis are joined together by bone.

What about the bone marrow cavities? Your bones are now much larger than they were when you were a baby. And as you continue to grow, they will get larger still. There was room for only a tiny marrow cavity in each bone when you were first born. If growth of bones meant just adding new solid bone to the ends, the marrow cavities could never get any bigger than they were when you were a baby. Yet the marrow cavities in your bones run nearly the whole length of the bones.

The bone-building cells that make new bone tissue are called *osteoblasts.* Their name means "bone formers." Bone cells of another kind also play an important part in the growth of bones.

They are the *osteoclasts* (OSS-TEE-OH-CLASTS) or "bone breakers." Their job is to eat away bone tissue from the ends of the marrow cavities, so that these hollows inside the bones keep growing as long as the bones themselves do.

How tall are you? How tall do you think you will be when you are fully grown? This will depend on a number of things. If your father and mother are tall, there is a good chance that you will be tall too. For we inherit the tendency to grow tall or short just as we inherit blue or brown eyes, black or blond hair.

To a great extent, hormones control how much we grow and when we stop growing. One of the most important of these is *human growth hormone*. It is produced in the pituitary gland, a pea-sized structure just under the brain. If your pituitary gland does not make enough growth hormone, you might be a dwarf. If too much is produced, you may become a giant. Basketball players who are more than seven feet tall probably had an unusually high amount of growth hormone in their blood in their growing years. Most people's pituitary glands produce just enough human growth hormone so that they can grow to a height between five and six feet.

The food we eat also helps to determine how tall we will grow. Eating enough protein is especially important during the growing years, as proteins are one of the basic building blocks for new tissues. Vitamins and minerals are important, too. As you grow taller, your bones are growing larger. You must have new supplies of calcium and phosphorus each day to build strong bones. You can get them by drinking milk and eating cheeses. But even if you are eating enough of these minerals in your foods, your body will not be able to use them properly unless you also have enough of certain vitamins, especially vitamin D. This vitamin helps the body to absorb calcium and phosphorus from food in the intestines. It is formed by cells in our skin when it is exposed to the sun. But in the winter, we do not go outdoors very much, and when we do we usually cover most of our skin with heavy clothing. Before doctors realized how important vitamin D is for normal growth, many children used to suffer from a disease called *rickets*. Their growing bones did not have enough minerals in them, and they became so soft that they bent out of shape. Rickets can be cured by taking extra doses of vitamin D, with a diet that has plenty of calcium and phosphorus. Your parents probably had to take a dose of cod liver oil each day. (Fish oils are rich in vitamin D.) Now vitamin D is usually added to milk, so that you get all the important bone builders at the same time.

The amount your bones will grow also depends

to some degree on how much exercise you get. The more stress that is put on a bone, the more it will grow. One scientist took two groups of baby rats and fed hard food to one group and soft food to the other. Both diets had the same amount of nourishment. But the rats that had to chew more developed slightly larger heads and faces, and their head and jaw bones were quite a bit heavier. Athletes usually develop much stronger and heavier bones than people who do not get much exercise. But if a person is kept in bed for a long time, his bones become thinner and weaker. Calcium salts are carried away by the blood, and the bones themselves actually become smaller. When the person gets up again, he may be in some danger of breaking his bones, until they have had a chance to grow strong again. One problem that is worrying space scientists is the effect of weight-lessness on the astronauts' bones. Without the pull of gravity, minerals are dissolved out of the bones and lost from the body. When astronauts go on long flights or stay in orbit for long periods, during which there is little or no gravity pulling on them, their bones become weak, and the fine balance of minerals in their blood may be upset. Space physicians are now studying these effects and trying to devise exercises that will keep the astronauts' bodies in good condition and keep their bones from wasting away.

Draw a picture of a man, standing up straight. Does it look "natural," or does it seem to be a little bit out of proportion? Take a ruler and measure the length of the head in your drawing, the length of the trunk of the body, and the lengths of the arms and legs. Figure out what fraction each part is of the total height of the figure. Now have someone measure your height and the lengths of your head, trunk, arms, and legs. Figure out the fractions for your body parts. Measure around your head with a tape measure, too. Do the same thing with your mother and father. Do you have a baby brother or sister? Or does a family that you know have a baby that you could measure? How do the height fractions of different people compare with the picture you drew? How do they compare with each other?

You were probably surprised to find that the baby's head is nearly as large as yours, and your head is nearly as large as your parents'. Yet you are much taller than a baby, and your parents are still taller than you. How could the proportions change so much?

The bones of the body do not all grow at the same rate. The skull grows rather slowly, while the long bones grow more rapidly. The bones of the arms and legs grow faster than the bones of the trunk. Gradually the proportions of the body change, and the length of the head takes a much

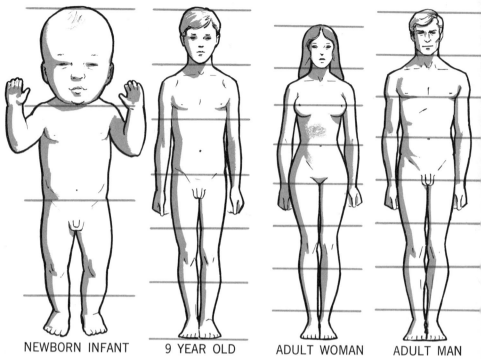

NEWBORN INFANT   9 YEAR OLD   ADULT WOMAN   ADULT MAN

The proportions of the body change as a child grows.

smaller fraction of the whole length of the body than it did at birth.

During your growing years, you do not always grow at the same rate. Has your mother kept a height record for you? If you examine the record, you will see that in some years you added barely an inch to your height, while in other years you may have grown three or four inches or even more. A big "growth spurt" will probably come during adolescence, when your body is changing from a child into an adult. During that time sex hormones work with the growth hormone to help your body grow. These sex hormones are responsible for the differences between the skeleton of a man and that of a woman. The male sex hormones, called *androgens* (AN-DROH-JENZ), help the bones to grow strong and thick. They cause the shoulder bones to grow broader. Female sex hormones, the *estrogens* (ESS-TROH-JENZ), tend to make the hip bones broader. In a woman, the space between the hip bones, the *pelvic cavity*, is wider than it is in a man. When she has a baby, it will be able to be born much more easily than it would if it had to squeeze through the narrow pelvic cavity of a man's body. Now, the trunk of your body probably is shaped like a rectangle. But when you are fully grown, if you are a boy, it will look more like a triangle standing on its point ($\triangledown$), or a triangle standing on its base ($\triangle$), if you are a girl.

Is the tallest child in your class a girl or a boy? What about the smallest? How many of each sex are taller than average? Before *puberty* (PEW-BER-TEE), the development of the sex organs, boys and girls of the same age are usually about the same height. But most men are taller than most women. Why is this so? The reason is that puberty usually comes later in boys than in girls. Before puberty, the legs grow faster than the trunk, but after the sexual development is complete, the growth of the long bones soon stops. So boys have a year or two more "growing time."

Even after you have reached your full height,

your bones will not lose all their ability to grow. Although bones seem to be unchanging, they are living tissues. Like the other tissues of the body, parts of the bones are constantly being built up and broken down. Normally these two processes just balance each other, and the bones seem to be unchanged. But under some conditions, one process, either buildup or breakdown of bone, may go faster than the other. Your bones will get stronger and thicker if you do a lot of heavy work or exercise, even after you are an adult. If you break a bone, the broken ends will grow together and heal the fracture. In fact, if a broken bone should heal together crookedly, an X-ray may show no signs of the mistake a few years later. Osteoblasts build up one part of the bone, while osteoclasts are eating away another, until it looks perfectly normal. The bone repair systems do not work as well in older people, and a thickened region may remain where a broken bone has healed.

After you are fifty or so, the breakdown of bone may be slightly faster than the buildup of new bone. People tend to get a little shorter after this age, and their bones may become lighter and weaker. The bones of very old people may break so easily that when you hear of someone who has "fallen and broken his hip," the reverse, may really have happened—his bone was so weakened that it broke, and then he fell down.

8
Animal Skeletons

Which are more alike: a bird's wing and an insect's wing, or a bird's wing and your arm?

A bird's wing and an insect's wing are both used for flying. They provide a surface that air currents can push against and help provide the lift that keeps the animal up in the air. Both birds and insects flap their wings to provide the thrust that moves them through the air.

But a bird's wing and an insect's wing are actually constructed quite differently. The bird's wing is made of flesh, with a rich supply of blood vessels. It has an inner framework of bone, which is attached to the rest of its skeleton in much the same way that your arm bones are attached to the rest of your skeleton. The insect's wings are made of a thin membrane, stretched across a network of thin, wire-like structures. It is built rather like a kite. It does not contain any blood vessels, nor any bones.

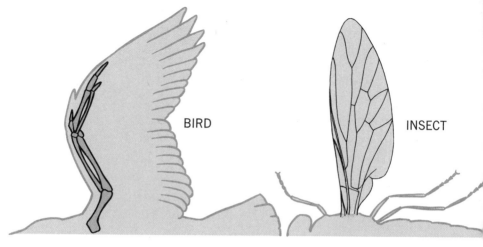

BIRD

INSECT

Both wings are used for flying, but their inner structures are very different.

Scientists call structures like the bird's wing and the insect's wing *analogous* (A-NAL-UH-GUS) *structures*. They do the same kind of job, but they may be built quite differently.

Can you think of other examples of analogous structures in the animal world? One example is the tail flukes of the whale and the tail of a fish. Both these structures help the animal to swim, but they are built differently, and they even work differently. The whale's tail flukes are horizontal, and they move up and down. The fish's tail is vertical, and it moves back and forth. Another example of analogous structures is the insect eye and the human eye. Both do the job of seeing the outside world, but the human eye contains one large lens, while the insect eye is a mosaic of tiny lenses—hundreds or even thousands of them. What other examples of analogous structures can you think of?

If you look at an X-ray picture of a bird's wing and a man's arm, you will find that their bony frameworks are surprisingly similar. In the upper part of each is a single, thick humerus. Below the elbow joint both the man and the bird have a pair of thinner long bones, the radius and the ulna. Then come the wrist bones, the carpals. The hand and finger bones, the metacarpals and phalanges, are rather different in the man and bird, but that is to be expected, considering what they can do. The bones at the end of the bird's "arm" provide the framework for the tips of its wings, while the bones at the end of a man's arm are the framework for a hand that can skillfully accomplish an almost endless variety of tasks.

Scientists have a name for structures like the bird's wing and the human arm. They are called

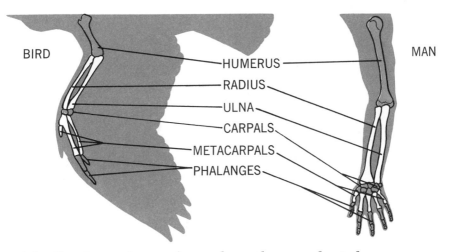

A bird's wing and a man's arm have the same basic bone structure.

homologous (нон-MOLL-uh-gus) *structures.* They are very similar in the way they are made, but they may be used for quite different tasks.

The group of vertebrates, animals with backbones, is filled with examples of homologous structures. Look at the drawing of the bones of the forelimbs of the frog, the bird, the cat, the horse, the bat, the whale, and man. The shapes of the bones vary—the whale has arm bones that are very thick in comparison with their length, while the bones of the bat are much more slender for their length than a man's. But the basic kinds of bones—humerus, radius and ulna, carpals, metacarpals, and phalanges—are all there in each case.

Look at your hand. You have four fingers that all point in just about the same direction, and a thumb that is set off at an angle to the rest of the hand. These are the five *digits* (DIDJ-ITS). Touch the tip of your thumb to the tips of each of the other fingers in turn. Now try to do the same thing with your forefinger. Try it with your little finger. The human hand has something that the paws of very few other animals have: an *opposable thumb.* The arrangement of bones and muscles of the hand permit the thumb to move against the fingers, like the opposite sides of a hinge. A hand with an opposable thumb can grip things much more firmly and securely than it could if all five digits were pointing in the same direction. The joint at the

52

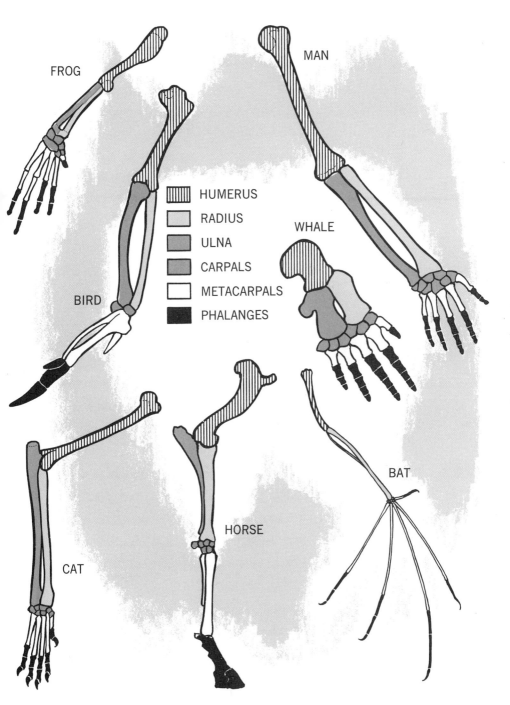

FROG

MAN

WHALE

BIRD

HUMERUS
RADIUS
ULNA
CARPALS
METACARPALS
PHALANGES

BAT

CAT

HORSE

Homologous bone structures show how animals are related.

base of the thumb permits such free movement that the hand can perform extremely delicate tasks. You can pick up a tiny grain of sand between the tips of your thumb and forefinger.

Fold your thumbs under and have someone tape them to the palms of your hands with strips of adhesive tape. Now try to do some of the things that you normally do with ease. Pick up a book, open it, and turn the pages. Try to write with a pencil. Try to eat something with a spoon or fork. Try to peel a banana. How awkward it is to do things without a thumb. With your thumbs taped down, your hands are very much like the front paws of a dog or cat. Look closely at the picture of the cat's hand bones. If you have a pet cat or dog, compare its front paw with the picture. There are separate bones for four complete fingers and a thumb. But the thumb is rather small, and its bones are shaped so that it cannot be opposed to the fingers, as our thumb can. A cat's thumb shows as just a small structure on the inner side of its paw. It is not of very much use, and the cat cannot pick things up in its paws as we can. Instead, it usually uses its mouth to pick up and carry things.

Look again at the homologous forelimbs on page 53. The frog, the cat, the bat, the whale, and the man all have the bones of five digits. But the "hand" of a bird shows the bones of only the first three digits. And a horse walks on a single toe on each foot. The bones that formed the third digit are greatly thickened and strengthened. Some of the bones from the second and fourth digits can be seen as tiny splints that help to support the leg. And the bones of the first and fifth digits are not there at all.

There are some examples of structures that are both analogous and homologous. One pair is the wing of the bird and the wing of the bat. Both help the animal to fly, and they have a similar basic structure. Can you think of any other examples of this kind?

Some homologous structures do not show on the outside. They are revealed only when the animal's skeleton is examined. Did you know that you have tail bones? The fused vertebrae at the end of your spine, called the *coccyx* (COCK-siks), are homologous to the tail bones of lizards, mice, and other animals with tails. Snakes and whales do not have legs, but their skeletons include hip and leg bones similar to the pelvis and femur of their vertebrate relatives. The study of homologous structures has helped scientists to learn and understand how animals are related.

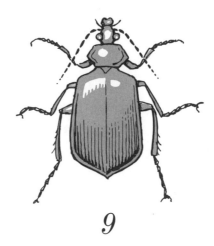

9

Skeletons on the Outside

Did you ever step on a beetle? If you did not step very hard, the insect may simply have gotten up and scooted away as soon as you lifted your foot. But if you did apply a great deal of force, enough to kill the beetle, you may have noticed a cracking sound. You had broken the beetle's suit of armor.

An insect's outer covering is similar in a number of ways to the suits of armor that were worn by knights in the Middle Ages. It is a hard tough covering that protects the insect from injury. It is made of many plates, jointed together. If it were not for these many joints, the insect would not be able to move at all. Its "armor" covering would keep it rigidly in place like a statue.

An insect's outer covering is called the *cuticle* (CUE-TIH-KL). It is made of a substance called

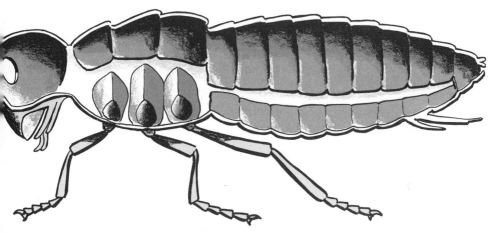

Human muscles are attached to the outside of bones; insect muscles are attached to the inside of the chitin skeleton.

chitin (KYE-TIN). Chitin is a *polysaccharide* (POLLY-SACK-A-RYDE), a chemical made of many sugar units joined together, and it is joined with various proteins. It is formed by the insect's skin cells, in much the same way that our bone cells produce the nonliving substance of bone. Chitin is an amazing substance. It is flexible and light, but it is very tough, and very few chemicals can harm it. In parts of the insect's cuticle that do not need to be flexible, the proteins form a tough, leathery substance something like your fingernails. In the joints, a rubbery substance makes the cuticle even more flexible. The insect's whole body is covered with an outer layer of wax that helps to keep the insect from getting wet and also helps to keep it from losing moisture from its body.

The cuticle covers every part of the insect's

body, and even lines some of its internal organs. This is the insect's skeleton. Man and the other vertebrates have a skeleton of bones on the inside of the body, an *endoskeleton*. But insects are *invertebrates*, animals without backbones. And like a number of the other invertebrates, they have a skeleton-on-the-outside, an *exoskeleton*.

The insect's skeleton is thus made in the form of a series of tubes, and it is amazingly strong for its weight. (A hollow tube is nearly as strong as a solid bar of the same diameter, and it is much lighter.) The soft tissues of the insect's body are packed

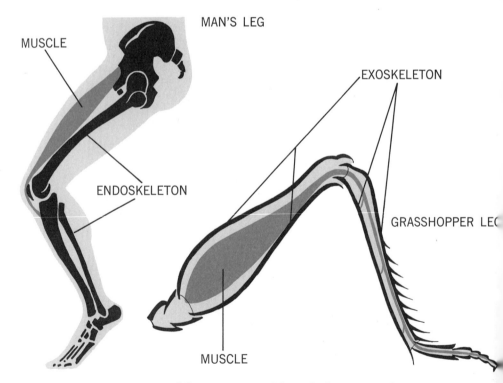

An insect could not move if his skeleton-on-the-outside were not jointed.

inside the exoskeleton, and are not only supported but also protected by it.

Muscles work with the insect's chitin skeleton to help it move, just as muscles work with your skeleton of bone to help you move. But your muscles are attached to the outsides of your bones. The insect's muscles, like all the rest of its body, are inside its chitin skeleton, and so they are attached to the inside of the skeleton. When the insect's muscles contract, they pull on the skeleton and cause the body parts to move.

A skeleton on the outside has a number of advantages. It provides the insect with both support and protection, and also helps to keep it from losing too much water. But a suit of armor has some built-in disadvantages. The knights of old wore such heavy armor that they had to be lifted onto their horses. If a knight was unseated during a battle, he could not climb back onto his horse by himself. He had to continue the fight on foot. Chitin is much lighter than steel, but if an insect grew very large —the size of a man—its suit of armor would be so thick and heavy that it would have trouble moving around. That is one reason why most insects do not grow larger than an inch or two.

Another disadvantage of a built-on suit of armor is that it does not leave the body any room to grow. Imagine what would happen if part of your arm were enclosed in a plaster cast; the type that the doctor puts on if you break a bone. The cast would protect your arm from harm, but what if the doctor did not take it off after a month or two? After a while the cast would feel very tight. The flesh around the cast would start to bulge out as your arm continued to grow. In time the cast might become so tight that it pressed on your blood vessels and stopped the circulation. Now what would happen if most of your body were covered with a plaster cast? You would burst!

In a way, that is exactly what a growing insect does. As it grows, its chitin "overcoat" becomes tighter and tighter. After a time, the skin begins to form a new layer of chitin, under the old cuticle. When the new cuticle is fully formed, the insect's old exoskeleton bursts, and the insect wriggles out. This shedding of the old outer covering is called

A Mayfly sheds its tight exoskeleton.

molting. After an insect molts, its new cuticle is still very soft. It draws as much air into its body as it can and puffs itself up. Now there is a larger mold for the new cuticle to harden over. The new exoskeleton will provide more room for growth.

An insect molts a number of times during its life, and these are times of special danger. The new cuticle is soft and pale. Air hardens it, just as exposure to air "sets" many glues and resins. But this process takes a few hours. During that time, the insect does not have a protective suit of armor, and its soft body may be pounced upon by some enemy—a bird or mouse or some other insect.

Skeletons on the outside that serve as suits of armor are found among many of the invertebrates, particularly those that live in the water. Water helps to hold things up. (You can float in the water, but you are much too heavy to float in air.) Animals that live in the water can have much heavier exoskeletons than land animals, and they can grow much larger, for the water helps to support them.

Lobsters and crabs are *crustaceans* (CRUS-TAY-SHANZ), close relatives of the insects, and their bodies are also covered with a cuticle. This cuticle is made into a hard shell by deposits of calcium salts. Indeed, most of the weight of a lobster's shell is the mineral lime that it contains. When a lobster or crab is getting ready to molt, some of the calcium salts are dissolved out of its cuticle. The old shell

The sea water helps to hold up the heavy exoskeletons of these invertebrates.

is softened and splits down the back. The crustacean crawls out and grows very rapidly for a short time. Then it grows a new cuticle, which hardens as calcium salts are deposited in it. Until its new shell is formed, the crustacean is very weak and can hardly move about.

Snails and clams also have a limy outer shell that protects and supports the soft tissues of their bodies. But they have a neat solution to the dangers of molting. As they grow, they simply add more shell around the outer edge of the old one. In this way, they never have to molt at all.

10

Clues to the Past

When a human skeleton is dug up and the police suspect that a murder many have been committed, they may find help in the Anthropology Department of the local university. After studying the bones, a physical anthropologist can tell whether the victim was a man or woman, how old he was when he died, and when the death occurred. He may be able to tell what caused the death, and he can reconstruct the person's general appearance—his height and weight, and even the features of his face—with startling accuracy. With this information, the detectives have a good start on their investigation of the crime.

The anthropologist develops his sleuthing skill by studying the bones of ancient men and piecing together the stories they tell. (*Anthropology* means "the study of man.") These bones, and the bones of animals that lived thousands and even millions of years ago, hold important clues to the history of life on our planet Earth.

Bones are the hardest parts of the body. When an old cemetery is dug up, bare skeletons are found in the graves. The soft flesh on the bodies that were buried there has decayed, and even the wood of the coffins may be gone, but the bones still seem unchanged. Yet if enough years go by, the minerals can be washed out of bones by the water and acids in the soil, and the bones themselves may disappear. How, then, do *paleontologists* (PAYL-EE-ON-TOL-O-JISTS), scientists who study the remains of ancient creatures, have anything left to study?

The remains of ancient creatures, called *fossils* (FOSS-ILZ), can be preserved in various ways. In some caves, particularly in desert regions where the air is very dry, the bodies of animals may be covered over with soil or rocks that have fallen from the roof of the cave. People living in the caves may bury their dead there. And in these sheltered places the bones may remain undisturbed until someone happens to dig in the cave. Sometimes animals are trapped in quicksand, in great pits of sticky tar, under rockfalls, or flows of hot lava from volcanoes, or in the moving ice of glaciers. Their bones, or even whole bodies, may be preserved there.

As the years go by, dust and soil are blown about and carried by flooding rivers. A new layer of soil

Fossils may be formed in various ways.

builds up over the bodies of the buried animals, and new plants begin to grow. They in turn die and are covered by new layers of soil. Many years go by—hundreds, thousands, millions of years. The buried layers of soil turn into rock. Bones and shells and other hard parts of animals' bodies may be preserved in these rocks. Waters flowing underground may dissolve parts of these remains, leaving spaces in the rocks like the hollows in a mold. This is a very slow process, and the softest parts dissolve first. After a hollow is formed, minerals may be deposited in it, filling the hollow just as you fill a mold with plaster of Paris. Slowly a rock model or *cast* is formed, which is a nearly perfect copy of the original form. If it was a bone, for example, the rock cast may even show the marks where the muscles of the living animal were attached to the bone. Casts such as these are another important kind of fossil that paleontologists study. The petrified forest in Arizona is an area of more than a hundred square miles, filled with stone casts of trees that lived long ages ago.

How can paleontologists tell how old fossils are? There are various ways. First of all, as the soil builds up, year after year, and then the buried parts turn into rock, layers or *strata* (STRAY-ᴛᴜʜ) are formed. In cuts deep into the earth, such as the mile-deep Grand Canyon carved out by the Colorado River, these strata can clearly be seen as bands of different-colored rocks. Each stratum contains fossils of animals and plants that lived

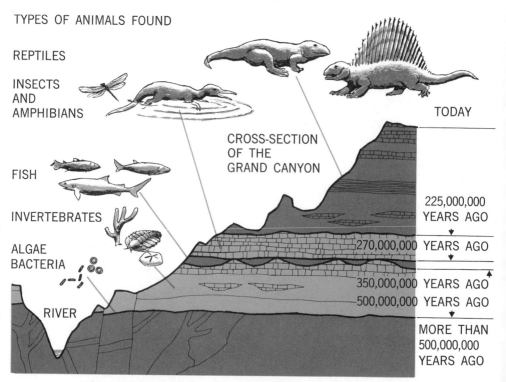

TYPES OF ANIMALS FOUND

REPTILES

INSECTS
AND
AMPHIBIANS

FISH

INVERTEBRATES

ALGAE
BACTERIA

RIVER

CROSS-SECTION
OF THE
GRAND CANYON

TODAY

225,000,000
YEARS AGO

270,000,000 YEARS AGO

350,000,000 YEARS AGO

500,000,000 YEARS AGO

MORE THAN
500,000,000
YEARS AGO

The record in the rocks of the Grand Canyon tells about life of the past.

during the period when its soil was still uncovered. The strata closest to the surface are usually the most recent, and the deepest strata are usually the oldest. Under your house there may be buried the foundation of a house built by frontier settlers, and beneath that the remains of an Indian camp. Still lower may be the bones of woolly mammoths, or even dinosaurs that roamed the lands long before there were any men alive.

Scientists have measured the rate that soil builds up, and so the depth of the strata gives them a guide to the age of the fossils that they contain. But the order and depth of the strata gives only a very rough guide. For during the long history of the earth, the surface of the land has changed many times. Great mountains have been raised up, and other mountains have been worn away by the wind and water. Great seas have been replaced by deserts, and lands have been washed into the oceans. In some areas, thousands or millions of years may be missing from the story of the strata, and some of the strata that remain may be folded or pushed out of place. For more accurate dates, some kind of "clock" is needed, a clock that can work independently of wind or water, heat or cold.

Scientists have found a number of clocks to use for dating the rocks of the earth and the fossils that they contain: radioactive substances. Remember that radioactive isotopes are unstable forms of the chemical elements that gradually break down, giving out energy in the form of radiations. The rate at which a radioactive isotope decays is always the same for that particular isotope. It is not changed by heat or cold or pressure, dryness or moisture, or practically any other influence. The radioactive "clocks" tick on evenly, regardless of the weather or other conditions on earth.

Many radioisotopes decay very rapidly. They have half-lives measured in weeks, or days, hours, or minutes, or even fractions of a second. These would not be very good "clocks" for measuring the age of ancient remains, for they disappear too quickly. Even strontium 90, which can stay in bones for so many years that it is a danger to our health, would not be very useful if we wanted to measure times of hundreds, thousands, or millions of years. But there are some isotopes that are very convenient for paleontologists to use. One of these is uranium 238. Uranium is a mineral found in rocks. In a concentrated form it is used in atomic bombs, but there is so little of it in rocks that its radiations cannot hurt us in its natural form. Uranium 238 has a half-life of four-and-a-half billion years. It breaks down to form another isotope that is also unstable. This isotope in turn decays, and so on in a series of steps until a stable form of lead, lead 206, is reached. Lead 206 is not radioactive, but it is not the normal form of lead. The only amounts of this isotope that are present in rocks are those that were formed from the decay of uranium 238. By measuring the amounts of uranium 238 and lead 206 in a sample of rock, scientists can figure out just how long ago the rock was formed. And the age of the rock tells them the age of the fossils that it contains.

Uranium 238 and some other radioisotopes with very long half-lives, measured in billions of years, are useful for dating very old samples. To date fossils that are more recent, less than about fifty thousand years old, scientists often use carbon 14, a form of the element carbon that has a half-life of 5770 years. Carbon is a very common element. It is found in the air we breathe, in the form of carbon dioxide, and it is a vital part of the body of every living thing on the earth. Proteins, carbohydrates, fats, and nucleic acids—the major chemicals of life—all are built from chains and rings of carbon atoms. Some radioactive carbon 14 is formed when the carbon dioxide in the upper atmosphere is hit by cosmic rays. And so the carbon dioxide that we breathe in contains a small amount of the radioactive form. Scientists believe that this amount has been about the same through most of the earth's history.

In your body, carbon 14 is constantly breaking down. But you are breathing in new carbon dioxide all the time. And so the relative amount of carbon

A skilled paleontologist can reconstruct missing parts of fossils.

14 in your tissues—including the bones—is about the same as that in the air. When an animal dies, it does not take in any more carbon by breathing. No more carbon will be added to its bones. As years go by, the amount of the stable form of carbon in the animal's bones will stay the same. But the carbon 14 will continue to decay, and so its amount will decrease. By measuring the amounts of the two forms of carbon in a sample of bone, and comparing them to the relative amounts in living bone, a scientist can determine how long ago the animal died.

The fossils that have been found are only a very tiny fraction of all the animals and plants that have lived on our planet. And so the study of fossils is like trying to put together a giant jigsaw puzzle, of which most of the pieces are missing. Even so, scientists have learned a great deal about the story of life on Earth. A paleontologist does not even need a whole skeleton to tell him what an animal looked liked. From a piece of a jawbone, he can figure out what the rest of the jaw must have looked like. The shape of the jaw will tell him things about the shape of the skull, and the neck and shoulders. Working carefully with broken bits of skeletons, he fills in the missing parts with clay. Markings on the fossil bones show him where the muscles were attached, and he adds layers of clay to reconstruct the muscles. With the shape of the muscles filled in, he knows how the skin and other tissues must have fit over them. Finally he has a model of how the animal looked when it was alive. Perhaps you have seen such reconstructions of ancient men and animals in a museum. Through the study of bones, paleontologists have learned about the great dinosaurs that once ruled the earth. They have found traces of the first birds and followed the development of mammals from tiny, mouse-like forms. They have found remains of ape-like creatures who may have been ancestors of the first men.

Index